Blockchain Gold Rush:

Surviving the Wild Wild West of Dectralization

By: Michael Ferguson

While every precaution has been taken in the preparation of this book, the publisher assumes no responsibility for errors or omissions, or for damages resulting from the use of the information contained herein.

BLOCKCHAIN GOLD RUSH: SURVIVING THE WILD WILD WEST OF DECENTRALIZATION

First edition. March 29, 2023.

ISBN: 979-8215540428

Written by Michael Ferguson.

Table of Contents

Chapter 1: Welcome to the Wild West of the Blockchain

Part 1: The Blockchain Basics: What It Is, How It Works, and Why It's So Wild

Welcome to the wild, wild world of the blockchain! You may have heard about this revolutionary technology that's taking the world by storm, but what exactly is it, and how does it work? In this chapter, we'll dive into the basics of the blockchain, exploring its origins, its defining characteristics, and its potential to transform the way we do business, manage our identities, and protect our data.

At its core, the blockchain is a digital ledger that records transactions in a secure and transparent way. Instead of relying on a central authority like a bank or government agency to verify and process transactions, the blockchain uses a decentralized network of computers to maintain and update a shared ledger of transactions. This means that no single entity has control over the network, and all participants have an equal say in the verification and processing of transactions.

But what makes the blockchain truly revolutionary is its ability to guarantee the integrity of the ledger without the need for a trusted intermediary. The blockchain achieves this through a process called "consensus," in which all participants in the network work together to verify and validate transactions. When a new transaction is submitted to the network, it's broadcast to all participants, who then use complex algorithms to verify the transaction and add it to the ledger. Once the transaction is confirmed and added to the ledger, it becomes a permanent part of the blockchain and can't be altered or deleted.

This process of consensus is what makes the blockchain so secure and resistant to fraud and tampering. Since every transaction is verified by a network of independent computers, it's virtually impossible for any single participant to manipulate the ledger. This is why the blockchain is often referred to as "trustless" – you don't have to trust anyone else in the network to ensure the integrity of the ledger.

But the blockchain isn't just about secure transactions. It also has the potential to transform a wide range of industries and applications, from finance and banking to supply chain management, digital identity, and more. By providing a secure, transparent, and decentralized platform for managing and verifying data, the blockchain has the potential to revolutionize the way we do business, interact with each other, and protect our most valuable assets.

Of course, with all this potential comes a certain amount of chaos and uncertainty. The blockchain is still a relatively new technology, and it's evolving rapidly. As a result, there are still many unanswered questions about its scalability, security, and potential impact on society. Additionally, the lack of central authority means that the blockchain can be a bit like the Wild West – there are few rules and regulations, and anything goes.

In the next section, we'll explore the joys and perils of decentralization on the blockchain, and why it's both exciting and a bit scary. We'll also look at the different types of consensus algorithms used on the blockchain, and how they contribute to the security and stability of the network. So buckle up and get ready for a wild ride – the blockchain is here, and it's not going away anytime soon!

Part 2: The Joys and Perils of Decentralization

Welcome back to the wild, wild world of the blockchain! In the previous section, we explored the basics of the blockchain, from its decentralized network to its secure and transparent ledger. But as we mentioned, with all this potential comes a certain amount of chaos and uncertainty. In this section, we'll explore the joys and perils of decentralization on the blockchain, and why it's both exciting and a bit scary.

Let's start with the joys of decentralization. One of the most exciting aspects of the blockchain is its ability to create a truly peer-to-peer network, where individuals can transact directly with each other without the need for intermediaries. This means that people can transfer money, buy and sell goods and services, and even manage their digital identities without relying on banks, governments, or other centralized institutions.

In a way, the blockchain is like the digital version of the Wild West – a place where pioneers can strike out on their own and build something new and exciting. But like the Wild West, the blockchain is also a place where anything goes, and where the rules can be a bit murky. This can create some perils for those who venture into this uncharted territory.

One of the biggest perils of decentralization on the blockchain is the lack of regulation. Without a central authority to enforce rules and standards, there's no guarantee that participants in the network will behave ethically or responsibly. This has led to some wild and wacky situations on the blockchain, from scams and Ponzi schemes to bizarre and often illegal activities.

For example, there have been instances of people using the blockchain to sell drugs, weapons, and other illegal goods and services. There have also been cases of hackers exploiting vulnerabilities in the blockchain to steal money or disrupt the network. And then there are the scams – fraudulent schemes that lure people into investing in fake cryptocurrencies or other bogus projects.

But despite these perils, many people still find the blockchain an exciting and exhilarating place to be. In fact, some see the lack of regulation as a feature, not a bug – a way to break free from the constraints of traditional institutions and create something truly new and innovative.

So how do we navigate the joys and perils of decentralization on the blockchain? One of the key factors is education. As with any new technology, it's important to understand the risks and benefits before diving in headfirst. This means doing your own research, asking questions, and seeking out trusted sources of information.

Another factor is community. The blockchain is built on the idea of collaboration and cooperation, and many participants in the network are passionate about helping others navigate the sometimes-treacherous waters of decentralization. By connecting with like-minded individuals, you can find support, guidance, and a sense of belonging in this exciting new world.

Finally, it's important to remember that the blockchain is still evolving. As we mentioned earlier, the lack of regulation means that the blockchain can be a bit like the Wild West – a place where anything goes and where the rules are constantly changing. This can be both exciting and intimidating, but it's also an opportunity to be part of something truly revolutionary.

So, whether you're a seasoned blockchain veteran or a newcomer to this exciting new world, remember to embrace the joys and perils of decentralization. The blockchain may be wild, but it's also a place where anything is possible – and that's something worth celebrating.

Part 3: Mining for Gold: Understanding Proof of Work and Proof of Stake

Welcome back, blockchain adventurers! In the previous section, we explored the joys and perils of decentralization on the blockchain. But as you probably already know, there's more to the blockchain than just trading cryptocurrencies and avoiding scams. In this section, we'll dive into the heart of the blockchain – the process of mining – and explore the differences between proof of work and proof of stake.

First, let's start with a quick overview of what mining is. Mining is the process by which new transactions are verified and added to the blockchain ledger. This is done by solving complex mathematical equations, which requires a lot of computing power. The miners who are able to solve these equations are rewarded with new cryptocurrency tokens, which they can then sell or hold onto as an investment.

Now, let's talk about the two main methods of mining – proof of work and proof of stake.

Proof of work (PoW) is the original mining algorithm used by Bitcoin and many other cryptocurrencies. In this method, miners compete to solve complex mathematical equations, with the first miner to solve the equation receiving a reward in the form of new cryptocurrency tokens. This process requires a lot of computing power, which is why many miners join forces in pools to increase their chances of success.

While proof of work has been successful in creating a secure and decentralized network, it has some drawbacks. One of the biggest issues with proof of work is its energy consumption. As the equations become more complex, it requires more and more energy to solve them. This has led to concerns about the environmental impact of proof of work mining.

Enter proof of stake (PoS). This is a newer method of mining that was designed to address some of the drawbacks of proof of work. In proof of stake, miners are chosen based on the amount of cryptocurrency tokens they hold. Essentially, the more tokens you have, the more mining power you have.

In proof of stake, there is no need for miners to solve complex equations. Instead, they simply validate transactions based on the amount of cryptocurrency they hold. This means that proof of stake mining is much more energy-efficient than proof of work, as it doesn't require the massive amounts of computing power needed to solve complex equations.

So, which method of mining is better – proof of work or proof of stake? Well, that's a bit of a tricky question. Each method has its own benefits and drawbacks, and the best method for a particular blockchain depends on the specific goals and needs of the network.

One of the advantages of proof of work is its security. Because it requires so much computing power to solve the equations, it's very difficult for any one miner or group of miners to manipulate the network. This makes proof of work a good choice for networks that require a high degree of security, such as Bitcoin.

On the other hand, proof of stake is much more energy-efficient and environmentally friendly than proof of work. This makes it a good choice for networks that prioritize sustainability and energy efficiency, such as Ethereum.

In the end, the choice between proof of work and proof of stake comes down to the specific needs and goals of the network. Some networks may use a combination of both methods, or even experiment with new mining algorithms altogether.

So there you have it – an overview of the two main methods of mining on the blockchain. Whether you're a miner yourself or simply interested in the inner workings of the blockchain, understanding proof of work and proof of stake is key to navigating this exciting and ever-changing landscape.

Chapter 2: The Hackers Are Coming! Protecting Your Assets on the Blockchain

Part 1: Common cybersecurity threats and how to thwart them

Welcome back, blockchain adventurers! In the previous chapter, we explored the basics of the blockchain and the different methods of mining. Now, let's talk about something a little more ominous – the threat of cyber-attacks on the blockchain.

It's no secret that the blockchain has become a hotbed for cybercriminals looking to steal cryptocurrency and other digital assets. In fact, according to a recent report by CipherTrace, losses due to cryptocurrency theft, scams, and fraud totaled over $4.5 billion in 2019 alone. That's a staggering amount of money, and it's clear that cyber attacks on the blockchain are a real and growing threat.

So, what can you do to protect yourself and your assets on the blockchain? Well, the first step is understanding the common cybersecurity threats and how to thwart them. Let's dive in.

Phishing Scams

Phishing scams are one of the most common forms of cyber-attacks on the blockchain. In a phishing scam, the attacker will send you an email or message that appears to be from a legitimate source – such as a cryptocurrency exchange or wallet provider – asking you to provide your login credentials or other sensitive information.

To protect yourself from phishing scams, always double-check the sender's email address or website URL to make sure it's legitimate. Don't click on any links in the email or message – instead, manually type the website URL into your browser. And if something seems too good to be true – such as an offer for free cryptocurrency – it probably is.

Malware

Malware – or malicious software – is another common threat on the blockchain. Malware can take many forms, including viruses, trojans, and ransomware. Once installed on your computer, malware can steal your login credentials, monitor your activity, or even take control of your computer.

To protect yourself from malware, always keep your computer's antivirus software up to date. Don't download or install software from untrusted sources, and always double-check the legitimacy of any software before installing it.

Social Engineering

Social engineering is a technique used by cybercriminals to manipulate and deceive people into giving up sensitive information. This can take many forms, including phone scams, email scams, and even in-person scams.

To protect yourself from social engineering, always be skeptical of any unsolicited phone calls, emails, or messages asking for sensitive information. Don't give out personal or financial information unless you're absolutely sure it's legitimate.

Blockchain Specific Threats

While the above threats are common across all forms of digital technology, there are also some blockchain-specific threats to be aware of. These include:

- 51% attacks, in which an attacker gains control of over 50% of a blockchain's mining power and can manipulate the network.
- Smart contract vulnerabilities, in which flaws in a smart contract's code can be exploited to steal cryptocurrency.
- Wallet hacks, in which a hacker gains access to a cryptocurrency wallet and steals the contents.

To protect yourself from blockchain-specific threats, always use reputable exchanges and wallet providers, and be sure to keep your private keys and passwords safe and secure.

In conclusion, cyber attacks on the blockchain are a real and growing threat, but by understanding the common threats and taking proactive measures to protect yourself, you can help ensure that your assets stay safe and secure. Stay tuned for the next chapter, where we'll dive deeper into the world of blockchain cybersecurity and explore advanced techniques for keeping your assets safe.

Part 2: Passwords that pop: Creating a strong and memorable passphrase

Welcome back, blockchain adventurers! In the previous section, we explored the common cybersecurity threats on the blockchain and how to protect yourself from them. Now, let's focus on one of the most basic yet essential aspects of cybersecurity – passwords.

Passwords are the first line of defense against cyber attacks, and creating a strong and memorable passphrase is crucial for keeping your assets safe. Let's dive in and explore how to create passwords that pop!

Why Strong Passphrases Matter

First things first, let's talk about why strong passphrases matter. A weak password can be easily cracked by a hacker using brute force techniques, which involves trying every possible combination of letters, numbers, and symbols until they crack the code.

A strong passphrase, on the other hand, is much more difficult to crack. By using a combination of words, numbers, and symbols, you can create a passphrase that's both strong and memorable.

Creating a Strong Passphrase

So, how do you create a strong passphrase? Well, the key is to use a combination of words, numbers, and symbols that are memorable to you but difficult for others to guess.

One popular method is to create a passphrase by combining four or more random words. For example, "coffee table keyboard rainbow" or "bookshelf bicycle sunset garden." These phrases are easy to remember but difficult for hackers to guess.

Another method is to use a passphrase that's easy to remember but difficult for others to guess. For example, "ILove2RunInMyFreeTime!" or "MyDogIsTheBestPetInTheWorld#1." These passphrases include a combination of upper and lowercase letters, numbers, and symbols, making them difficult to crack.

Avoiding Common Password Mistakes

When creating a passphrase, it's important to avoid common password mistakes. For example, don't use easily guessable information, such as your name, birthdate, or address. These are the first things that hackers will try when attempting to crack your password.

Additionally, don't reuse passwords across multiple accounts. If one account is compromised, all of your accounts could be at risk. Instead, use a unique passphrase for each account.

Memorizing Your Passphrase

Once you've created a strong passphrase, it's important to memorize it. Avoid writing it down or storing it in an unencrypted file on your computer – these are easy targets for hackers.

Instead, use memory tricks such as acronyms or associations to help you remember your passphrase. For example, you could create an acronym from your passphrase – "CTKR" for "coffee table keyboard rainbow" – or associate it with a memorable image or story.

Using a Password Manager

If you're struggling to remember your passphrases or need to create unique passphrases for multiple accounts, consider using a password manager. Password managers are software applications that store and encrypt your passwords, allowing you to access them with a single master password.

When using a password manager, it's important to choose a reputable and secure option. Look for a password manager that uses end-to-end encryption, two-factor authentication, and has a strong track record of security.

In conclusion, creating a strong and memorable passphrase is essential for protecting your assets on the blockchain. By using a combination of words, numbers, and symbols, avoiding common password mistakes, and memorizing your passphrase, you can create a password that's both strong and easy to remember. And if you need help keeping track of multiple passphrases, consider using a password manager. Stay tuned for the next section, where we'll explore additional cybersecurity techniques for keeping your assets safe on the blockchain.

Part 3: Two-factor authentication: Why it's important and how to set it up

Welcome back, blockchain adventurers! In the previous section, we explored how to create strong and memorable passphrases to protect your assets on the blockchain. Now, let's dive into another essential aspect of cybersecurity – two-factor authentication.

What is Two-Factor Authentication?

Two-factor authentication, or 2FA, is an additional layer of security beyond just a username and password. 2FA requires a second factor, such as a code sent to your phone or a fingerprint scan, to verify your identity before granting access to your account.

Why is 2FA Important?

2FA is important because it provides an additional layer of security against cyber attacks. Even if a hacker were to obtain your password, they would still need access to your phone or other 2FA device to gain access to your account. This extra layer of security can prevent unauthorized access and protect your assets.

Setting Up 2FA

Now that we know why 2FA is important, let's explore how to set it up. The process varies depending on the platform you're using, but the general steps are as follows:

Step 1: Choose a 2FA Method

The first step is to choose a 2FA method that works for you. Popular options include:

- SMS authentication: A code is sent to your phone via text message.
- Authenticator app: An app on your phone generates a unique code that changes every few seconds.
- Hardware token: A physical device that generates a unique code.

Step 2: Enable 2FA on Your Account

Once you've chosen a 2FA method, the next step is to enable it on your account. This process varies depending on the platform, but typically involves going to your account settings and finding the 2FA section. From there, you'll be prompted to enter your phone number or other 2FA device and verify your identity.

Step 3: Verify Your Identity

After you've enabled 2FA on your account, you'll need to verify your identity to complete the setup process. This typically involves entering a code sent to your phone or generated by your 2FA device.

Best Practices for 2FA

To ensure maximum security, it's important to follow best practices when using 2FA. Here are a few tips:

- Use a unique 2FA method for each account.
- Keep your 2FA device secure and don't share it with others.
- Use a backup method, such as a recovery code or backup device, in case you lose access to your primary 2FA device.
- Regularly update your 2FA settings and review your account activity for any suspicious activity.

In conclusion, two-factor authentication is an essential aspect of cybersecurity on the blockchain. By adding an extra layer of security beyond just a password, you can protect your assets and prevent unauthorized access. Follow the steps outlined above to set up 2FA on your accounts and follow best practices for maximum security. Stay tuned for the next section, where we'll explore additional cybersecurity techniques for keeping your assets safe on the blockchain.

Part 4: The dangers of public Wi-Fi and how to stay safe

Greetings, fellow blockchain enthusiasts! In the previous section, we explored the importance of two-factor authentication and how to set it up. Now, let's delve into another cybersecurity threat that can jeopardize your assets on the blockchain – public Wi-Fi.

What is Public Wi-Fi?

Public Wi-Fi refers to wireless internet connections that are publicly accessible in places like coffee shops, airports, and hotels. While these connections can be convenient, they also pose significant security risks.

The Dangers of Public Wi-Fi

Hackers can easily intercept data transmitted over public Wi-Fi, including login credentials and sensitive information. This is because most public Wi-Fi connections are unsecured and don't encrypt data, making it easy for cybercriminals to access and steal.

How to Stay Safe on Public Wi-Fi

Fortunately, there are steps you can take to protect yourself and your assets when using public Wi-Fi. Here are a few tips:

1. Avoid Public Wi-Fi Whenever Possible

The simplest way to avoid the dangers of public Wi-Fi is to not use it at all. Whenever possible, use a secure and trusted internet connection, such as your home network or a mobile hotspot.

1. Use a Virtual Private Network (VPN)

If you must use public Wi-Fi, consider using a VPN. A VPN encrypts your data and creates a secure tunnel between your device and the internet, making it much harder for hackers to intercept your information.

1. Avoid Accessing Sensitive Information

When using public Wi-Fi, avoid accessing sensitive information like banking or cryptocurrency accounts. If you must access these accounts, use two-factor authentication and make sure the website is using HTTPS encryption.

1. Keep Your Devices Updated

Make sure your devices are up to date with the latest security patches and software updates. This can help prevent known vulnerabilities from being exploited by hackers.

1. Use Antivirus Software

Install antivirus software on your devices to help detect and prevent malware infections. Many antivirus programs also include features like firewalls and web filters that can help protect you on public Wi-Fi.

In conclusion, public Wi-Fi can be a significant threat to your cybersecurity on the blockchain. By following the tips outlined above, you can stay safe and protect your assets when using public Wi-Fi. Stay tuned for the next section, where we'll explore additional cybersecurity techniques for keeping your assets safe on the blockchain.

Chapter 3: Who Are You? Managing Your Digital Identity on the Blockchain

Part 1: The power of anonymity on the blockchain

Welcome back, my fellow blockchain enthusiasts! In the previous chapters, we explored the basics of blockchain technology, the importance of cybersecurity, and how to protect your assets on the blockchain. Now, let's turn our attention to a crucial aspect of the blockchain ecosystem – digital identity.

One of the key features of the blockchain is its ability to provide users with anonymity. In traditional financial transactions, the identity of the sender and receiver is known to the bank or financial institution processing the transaction. However, on the blockchain, transactions are processed anonymously using pseudonyms, which are randomly generated strings of characters.

The benefits of anonymity on the blockchain

Anonymity on the blockchain can provide several benefits, including:

1. Privacy: Anonymity protects your identity and personal information from being exposed in the public domain. This is particularly important in an era where privacy concerns are on the rise.
2. Security: Anonymity on the blockchain provides an additional layer of security by making it difficult for hackers to trace and access your information.
3. Freedom: Anonymity allows for greater freedom of speech and expression, as users can express their opinions and ideas without fear of retribution or censorship.
4. Inclusivity: Anonymity on the blockchain allows individuals who may be marginalized or underrepresented in society to participate and transact freely without fear of discrimination or prejudice.

However, anonymity on the blockchain can also have its downsides. It can make it difficult to enforce laws and regulations, as transactions can be conducted without any oversight or accountability. This has led to concerns about the use of the blockchain for illicit activities, such as money laundering and terrorism financing.

Managing your digital identity on the blockchain

While anonymity on the blockchain can provide many benefits, it's important to manage your digital identity carefully. Here are some tips for managing your digital identity on the blockchain:

1. Use pseudonyms wisely: When creating a pseudonym, choose something that is unique and not easily traceable back to your real identity.

2. Keep your private key secure: Your private key is the key to your digital identity on the blockchain. Make sure to keep it secure and don't share it with anyone.

3. Use multi-signature wallets: multi-signature wallets require multiple signatures to authorize a transaction, providing an additional layer of security.

4. Be mindful of the information you share: While anonymity can provide privacy and security, it's important to be mindful of the information you share on the blockchain. Don't reveal personal information or share sensitive data.

5. Stay up to date with the latest developments: The blockchain ecosystem is constantly evolving, and new technologies and practices are emerging all the time. Stay up to date with the latest developments and best practices for managing your digital identity on the blockchain.

Anonymity on the blockchain can provide many benefits, including privacy, security, freedom, and inclusivity. However, it's important to manage your digital identity carefully and be mindful of the information you share. Stay tuned for the next section, where we'll explore the importance of blockchain-based identity management solutions.

Part 2: The importance of creating a unique digital identity

Welcome back, my fellow blockchain enthusiasts! In the previous section, we explored the power of anonymity on the blockchain and how to manage your digital identity carefully. In this section, we'll dive deeper into the importance of creating a unique digital identity.

Chapter 3: Who Are You? Managing Your Digital Identity on the Blockchain

The importance of creating a unique digital identity

Creating a unique digital identity is an essential aspect of managing your presence on the blockchain. Your digital identity is your online persona, and it represents who you are in the digital world. It's a reflection of your values, beliefs, and interests, and it can have a significant impact on how you're perceived by others.

Here are some reasons why creating a unique digital identity is crucial:

1. Identity theft: Identity theft is a significant concern in the digital age. Hackers can use stolen personal information to commit fraud, steal money, or engage in other illicit activities. By creating a unique digital identity, you can protect your personal information and prevent identity theft.

2. Reputation management: Your digital identity can have a significant impact on your reputation. A strong digital identity can help you build trust and credibility with others, while a weak or inconsistent identity can damage your reputation.

3. Personal branding: Creating a unique digital identity can also help you establish a personal brand. A strong personal brand can help you stand out in a crowded marketplace, attract new opportunities, and achieve your career goals.

1. Social media: Social media platforms like Facebook, Twitter, and LinkedIn have become essential tools for networking, job searching, and marketing. By creating a unique digital identity, you can establish a consistent presence on these platforms and build your online network.

2. Blockchain-based identity management: Finally, creating a unique digital identity is critical for blockchain-based identity management solutions. These solutions use the blockchain to create secure and decentralized digital identities that can be used for a variety of purposes, including secure authentication, access control, and secure data sharing.

Here are some tips for creating a unique digital identity on the blockchain:

1. Choose a unique username: When creating a digital identity, choose a username that is unique and memorable. Avoid using common or easily guessable usernames.
2. Use a strong password: Use a strong, unique password that is difficult to guess. Don't reuse passwords or use easily guessable passwords like "password123."
3. Establish a consistent brand: Establish a consistent brand across all your digital channels, including your social media profiles, website, and blog.
4. Use secure identity management solutions: Use blockchain-based identity management solutions to create secure, decentralized digital identities that can be used for a variety of purposes.

In conclusion, creating a unique digital identity is essential for managing your presence on the blockchain. It can protect you from identity theft, help you establish a strong personal brand, and provide secure access to blockchain-based services. By following these tips, you can create a digital identity that is unique, secure, and reflects who you are in the digital world. Stay tuned for the next section, where we'll explore the role of identity verification in the blockchain ecosystem.

Part 3: Keeping your identity safe: Best practices for staying anonymous on the blockchain

When it comes to managing your digital identity on the blockchain, one of the most important considerations is privacy. While the blockchain is often touted as a secure and anonymous system, the reality is that it is not foolproof, and users must take steps to protect their identity and keep their information safe.

There are a few key best practices that you should keep in mind when using the blockchain to ensure that your identity remains private and secure.

First and foremost, it is important to use a secure and anonymous wallet. There are a number of different wallet options available, but not all of them are created equal when it comes to privacy and security. Look for a wallet that uses strong encryption and allows for anonymous transactions, such as the ability to use multiple addresses.

Another important consideration is the use of pseudonyms. When creating a digital identity on the blockchain, it is best to use a pseudonym or handle rather than your real name. This can help to protect your identity and prevent others from tracing your transactions back to you.

It is also important to be careful about the types of information that you share on the blockchain. Avoid posting personal information, such as your address or phone number, and be cautious about sharing sensitive financial information.

When it comes to transactions on the blockchain, it is also important to be mindful of the public nature of the blockchain. While transactions themselves may be anonymous, the fact that they are recorded on the blockchain means that they are publicly visible. As such, it is important to be careful about the types of transactions that you engage in and to be mindful of the potential implications of those transactions being visible to others.

Finally, it is important to keep your computer and other devices secure when using the blockchain. Make sure that you have up-to-date antivirus software installed and use a VPN to encrypt your internet connection. Additionally, be careful about the types of websites and apps that you use when accessing the blockchain, as some may be less secure than others.

By following these best practices, you can help to ensure that your digital identity remains safe and anonymous on the blockchain. While there is no guaranteed way to prevent all forms of identity theft or fraud, taking these steps can significantly reduce your risk and give you greater peace of mind when using this powerful technology.

Chapter 4: A Wallet That Won't Weigh You Down: Securing Your Blockchain Wallet

Part 1: The ins and outs of blockchain wallets

As more and more people begin to explore the world of cryptocurrency, the need for a secure and reliable blockchain wallet has become increasingly important. A blockchain wallet is essentially a digital wallet that is used to store and manage various types of digital assets, including cryptocurrencies like Bitcoin, Ethereum, and Litecoin.

At its core, a blockchain wallet is essentially a software application that allows users to interact with the blockchain network. Unlike traditional wallets that store physical currency, a blockchain wallet stores digital assets on the blockchain itself, which is a decentralized, distributed ledger that records all transactions on the network.

There are a few different types of blockchain wallets that are commonly used, each of which offers its own unique set of benefits and drawbacks. One of the most popular types of blockchain wallets is known as a hot wallet. A hot wallet is a wallet that is connected to the internet and is designed to allow for easy and convenient access to digital assets. These wallets are often used for day-to-day transactions, as they allow for quick and easy transfers of funds.

Another popular type of blockchain wallet is known as a cold wallet. A cold wallet is a wallet that is not connected to the internet and is designed to provide a high level of security for digital assets. These wallets are often used for long-term storage of digital assets, as they offer a greater degree of protection against hacking and other security threats.

Regardless of the type of wallet that you choose, it is important to understand that blockchain wallets are not like traditional wallets. Digital assets are stored on the blockchain itself, rather than in the wallet itself. The wallet simply provides a way to access and manage those assets on the network.

One of the most important considerations when choosing a blockchain wallet is security. Because digital assets are stored on the blockchain network, it is essential to choose a wallet that provides a high level of security and protection against hacking and other threats.

There are a few different security features that you should look for when choosing a blockchain wallet. One of the most important is two-factor authentication, which requires users to provide two different types of identification in order to access the wallet. This can include a password, a fingerprint scan, or another form of identification.

Another important security feature to look for is multi-signature support. Multi-signature support allows for multiple parties to sign off on transactions, which can help to prevent fraud and other security threats.

In addition to these features, it is also important to choose a blockchain wallet that is reputable and has a strong track record of security and reliability. Look for wallets that have been around for a while and have a large user base, as these are often the most reliable and secure options.

Overall, choosing the right blockchain wallet is an essential part of managing your digital assets. By understanding the ins and outs of blockchain wallets and choosing a wallet that provides a high level of security and protection, you can help to ensure that your digital assets remain safe and secure on the blockchain network.

Part 2: Hot vs. cold storage: Which is right for you?

When it comes to securing your blockchain wallet, one important consideration is whether to use hot or cold storage.

Hot storage refers to any wallet that is connected to the internet, while cold storage refers to wallets that are kept offline. Each option has its own benefits and drawbacks, and the choice ultimately depends on your specific needs and preferences.

Hot wallets are generally more convenient to use, as they allow you to easily access your funds from any device with an internet connection. However, because they are connected to the internet, they are also more vulnerable to hacking attempts and other security risks.

Cold wallets, on the other hand, are much more secure because they are not connected to the internet. This makes them ideal for storing large amounts of cryptocurrency for long periods of time. However, they are less convenient to use because they require physical access to the wallet itself in order to make transactions.

There are several types of hot and cold wallets available, each with their own unique features and benefits. Some popular hot wallets include online exchanges, mobile wallets, and desktop wallets. These wallets are often free to use and can be downloaded or accessed through a web browser.

Cold wallets, on the other hand, include hardware wallets, paper wallets, and even physical coins or tokens. Hardware wallets are small, USB-like devices that store your private keys offline, while paper wallets involve printing out your private keys on a piece of paper and storing it in a secure location. Physical coins or tokens are essentially physical representations of your cryptocurrency that can be kept in a safe or other secure location.

Ultimately, the type of wallet you choose will depend on your specific needs and preferences. If you plan on using your cryptocurrency frequently and need quick and easy access to your funds, a hot wallet may be the better option. If you plan on storing your cryptocurrency for long periods of time and want maximum security, a cold wallet may be the better choice.

Regardless of which type of wallet you choose, it's important to follow best practices for securing your funds, such as keeping your private keys in a secure location and enabling two-factor authentication wherever possible. By taking the necessary precautions, you can ensure that your blockchain wallet remains safe and secure.

Part 3: Securing your private keys: Best practices for keeping your wallet safe

Securing your private keys is essential for keeping your blockchain wallet safe. Private keys are essentially the password that allows you to access and manage your cryptocurrency, and if they fall into the wrong hands, you could be at risk of losing your funds.

To ensure the security of your private keys, there are several best practices you can follow:

1. Keep your private keys offline: One of the best ways to keep your private keys safe is to keep them offline. This can be done using a cold storage wallet, such as a hardware wallet or a paper wallet. By keeping your private keys offline, you can ensure that they are not vulnerable to hacking attempts or other security risks.

2. Use strong passwords: When creating a password for your wallet, be sure to use a strong and unique password that is difficult to guess. Avoid using common phrases or personal information, and consider using a password manager to generate and store complex passwords.

1. Enable two-factor authentication: Two-factor authentication is an extra layer of security that requires you to enter a code or use a physical device in addition to your password in order to access your wallet. This can help prevent unauthorized access to your funds.
2. Regularly back up your wallet: It's important to regularly back up your wallet in case your device is lost, stolen, or damaged. This can be done by exporting your private keys or using a backup feature built into your wallet software.
3. Keep your software up to date: It's important to keep your wallet software up to date with the latest security patches and updates. This can help prevent vulnerabilities and security risks.
4. Be cautious of phishing scams: Phishing scams are a common tactic used by hackers to steal private keys and other sensitive information. Be cautious of any unsolicited emails or messages asking for your private keys or other personal information.

By following these best practices, you can ensure the security of your private keys and keep your blockchain wallet safe. It's important to take the necessary precautions to protect your funds, as the decentralized nature of the blockchain means that there is no central authority to turn to in the event of a security breach.

Recovering from a lost or stolen blockchain wallet can be a daunting process, but it's important to know what steps you can take to try and recover your funds. Here are some best practices for recovering from a lost or stolen wallet:

1. Try to access your wallet using your backup: If you have backed up your wallet, try to access it using your backup. This may involve importing your private keys or using a recovery phrase provided by your wallet software.

1. Check if your funds have been moved: If you suspect that your wallet has been compromised, check the blockchain to see if any funds have been moved out of your wallet. If you can identify the address that the funds were moved to, you may be able to contact the owner of the address or report the transaction to the authorities.
2. Contact your wallet provider: If you are unable to access your wallet or if you suspect that it has been compromised, contact your wallet provider for assistance. They may be able to help you recover your funds or provide guidance on how to report the incident.
3. Report the theft to the authorities: If your wallet has been stolen, report the theft to the authorities as soon as possible. This can help you recover your funds and may also prevent the thief from stealing from others.
4. Consider using a professional recovery service: If you are unable to recover your funds using the above methods, you may consider using a professional recovery service. These services specialize in recovering lost or stolen funds and may be able to help you recover your funds for a fee.

It's important to note that recovering from a lost or stolen wallet can be a difficult and time-consuming process, and there is no guarantee that you will be able to recover your funds. To avoid the risk of losing your funds, it's important to take the necessary precautions to keep your wallet secure, such as using strong passwords, enabling two-factor authentication, and keeping your software up to date.

In conclusion, recovering from a lost or stolen blockchain wallet can be a challenging process, but there are steps you can take to try and recover your funds. By following best practices for wallet security and taking the necessary precautions, you can help reduce the risk of losing your funds and ensure that you are prepared in the event of a security breach.

Chapter 5: Going Beyond Bitcoin: Staying Safe While Using Blockchain-Based Apps and Platforms

Blockchain technology has grown beyond just being the underlying technology for cryptocurrencies like Bitcoin. Nowadays, blockchain is being used to develop a wide range of applications and platforms, from supply chain management to online voting and even gaming. The decentralized nature of blockchain makes it an attractive technology for developers who are looking to build trust and transparency into their applications.

These blockchain-based apps and platforms have the potential to revolutionize the way we interact with the digital world. They can provide us with more control over our personal data, create new opportunities for peer-to-peer transactions, and eliminate the need for intermediaries like banks and other financial institutions. However, as with any new technology, there are risks involved.

In this chapter, we will explore the rise of blockchain-based apps and platforms, the benefits they offer, and the potential risks associated with using them. We will also provide tips on how to stay safe while using these applications, so that you can enjoy the benefits of this exciting technology without putting yourself at risk. So, let's dive in!

Part 1: The rise of blockchain-based apps and platforms

Blockchain technology has given rise to a new wave of innovation, as developers and entrepreneurs seek to harness its potential to create new applications and platforms. The first blockchain-based application, Bitcoin, paved the way for a host of other applications that have since been developed using the same underlying technology. These applications range from supply chain management to online voting and even gaming, all of which aim to leverage the unique features of blockchain to create more secure, transparent, and efficient systems.

One of the most significant benefits of blockchain-based apps and platforms is their decentralized nature. Rather than relying on a centralized authority to manage and control the system, these applications are built on a decentralized network of nodes that work together to validate transactions and maintain the integrity of the network. This means that there is no single point of failure or vulnerability, making blockchain-based systems more resistant to attacks and less prone to errors and downtime.

Another key benefit of blockchain-based apps and platforms is the ability to create more secure and transparent systems. Because blockchain is based on a distributed ledger that is shared among all participants, it is very difficult for any one participant to manipulate the data or change the rules of the system. This makes blockchain-based systems more resistant to fraud and corruption and helps to ensure that all transactions are recorded accurately and transparently.

One of the most exciting applications of blockchain technology is in the realm of finance. Blockchain-based platforms like Ethereum have created a new class of digital assets called tokens, which can be used to represent a wide range of assets and values. These tokens can be bought, sold, and traded on decentralized exchanges, giving users more control over their financial assets and allowing them to participate in new forms of economic activity.

In addition to finance, blockchain technology is also being used in supply chain management, where it can help to create more transparency and efficiency in the movement of goods and products. By using blockchain to track the movement of goods from production to delivery, companies can reduce the risk of fraud and errors, and ensure that products are delivered on time and in the condition that they were promised.

Online voting is another area where blockchain technology has the potential to make a significant impact. By using blockchain to create a tamper-proof record of votes, online voting systems can provide a more secure and transparent way for people to participate in the democratic process. This could help to increase voter turnout and make elections more trustworthy and legitimate.

Overall, the rise of blockchain-based apps and platforms represents an exciting new frontier in technology. With their decentralized, secure, and transparent nature, these systems have the potential to revolutionize the way we interact with the digital world. However, as with any new technology, there are also risks involved. In the next part of this chapter, we will explore some of the potential risks associated with using blockchain-based apps and platforms and provide tips on how to stay safe while using them.

Part 2: The benefits and risks of using decentralized applications

Decentralized applications (Dapps) are becoming more and more popular as people seek to take control of their own data and transactions. However, like any new technology, Dapps come with their own set of benefits and risks. In this part of Chapter 5, we'll take a closer look at what Dapps are, what their benefits are, and what the potential risks are.

First, let's define what a Dapp is. A Dapp is a software application that is run on a blockchain. This means that the application is decentralized, and there is no central authority controlling it. All the data and transactions are recorded on the blockchain, which means that they are transparent and immutable.

One of the biggest benefits of Dapps is that they are decentralized. This means that there is no central authority controlling the data or transactions. This can be a huge benefit for users who are concerned about their privacy and security. Since there is no central authority, there is no need to worry about the data being hacked or manipulated by a third party.

Another benefit of Dapps is that they are often open source. This means that anyone can access the code and make improvements or modifications to it. This can lead to a community-driven development process that can help ensure that the Dapp is secure, efficient, and user-friendly.

However, there are also some potential risks associated with using Dapps. One risk is that the dApp may not be as secure as it appears. Since Dapps are often open source, it's possible that someone could introduce a vulnerability into the code. Additionally, since the Dapp is decentralized, there is no central authority that can oversee security measures.

Another risk of using Dapps is that they may not be as user-friendly as traditional apps. Since Dapps are often built on blockchain technology, they can be more complicated to use than traditional apps. This can be a barrier to adoption for some users.

Finally, there is the risk of losing access to your assets. Since Dapps are decentralized, there is no central authority that can help you recover your assets if you lose access to them. This means that it's important to take precautions to ensure that you don't lose access to your assets.

In conclusion, Dapps are an exciting new technology that offer a lot of benefits to users. They are decentralized, transparent, and often open source. However, there are also some potential risks associated with using Dapps. It's important to understand these risks and take precautions to ensure that you stay safe while using blockchain-based apps and platforms.

Part 3: Protecting your data: Best practices for using blockchain-based platforms

As with any technology, there are risks involved in using blockchain-based platforms. While the decentralized nature of blockchain makes it more secure in many ways, it's still important to take steps to protect your data and personal information. Here are some best practices to follow when using blockchain-based platforms:

1. Use a strong password and enable two-factor authentication: Just as with any online account, it's important to use a strong, unique password for your blockchain-based platform account. You should also enable two-factor authentication (2FA) if it's available. This will require you to enter a code sent to your phone or email in addition to your password when logging in, adding an extra layer of security.

1. Be cautious when sharing personal information: When using blockchain-based platforms, be cautious about sharing personal information such as your full name, address, or phone number. While some platforms may require this information for verification purposes, you should only share what is necessary and avoid providing unnecessary details.

2. Only use trusted platforms: Before using any blockchain-based platform, do your research to ensure that it's reputable and has a good track record. Check user reviews and ratings and look for information on the platform's security practices.

3. Keep your software up to date: Just as with any software, it's important to keep your blockchain-based platform up to date with the latest security patches and updates. This will help to ensure that any known security vulnerabilities are patched.

1. Use a hardware wallet for storing cryptocurrency: If you're using a blockchain-based platform that involves storing cryptocurrency, consider using a hardware wallet rather than storing your cryptocurrency on the platform itself. Hardware wallets are physical devices that store your private keys offline, making them less vulnerable to hacking or theft.

1. Be wary of phishing scams: Phishing scams are a common tactic used by cybercriminals to try to steal your personal information or login credentials. Be cautious of any unsolicited emails or messages and avoid clicking on links or downloading attachments from unknown sources.

2. Use a VPN when accessing blockchain-based platforms: When accessing blockchain-based platforms from public Wi-Fi networks or other unsecured connections, consider using a virtual private network (VPN) to encrypt your traffic and protect your data.

By following these best practices, you can help to protect your data and personal information when using blockchain-based platforms. While there are always risks involved with any technology, taking proactive steps to secure your accounts and devices can go a long way in mitigating those risks.

Part 4: Understanding smart contracts and the potential risks they pose

Smart contracts are a key feature of many blockchain-based platforms, allowing for automated execution of contractual terms between parties. While they offer numerous benefits, such as increased efficiency and reduced transaction costs, they also pose potential risks that users should be aware of.

One of the primary risks associated with smart contracts is their immutability. Once a smart contract is executed, it cannot be altered or reversed without the agreement of all parties involved. This means that if a mistake is made in the coding of the contract, or if one party fails to meet their obligations, it can be difficult or impossible to rectify the situation.

Another risk is the potential for bugs or vulnerabilities in the code of the smart contract. If a flaw is present in the code, it can be exploited by malicious actors to gain unauthorized access or control over the contract. This can result in a loss of funds or other assets, as well as damage to the reputation of the platform hosting the contract.

Furthermore, smart contracts may be subject to legal or regulatory risks. While they are designed to operate autonomously without the need for intermediaries, they may still be subject to laws and regulations governing contracts and financial transactions. This can create uncertainty and legal risks for users of smart contract-based platforms.

To mitigate these risks, users of smart contracts should take several precautions. First and foremost, it is important to thoroughly review the code of any smart contract before executing it. This can help identify potential flaws or vulnerabilities that could be exploited by attackers. Additionally, users should ensure that they fully understand the terms of the contract and any associated risks before agreeing to it.

Another important step is to use established, reputable platforms for executing smart contracts. These platforms typically have robust security measures in place to protect against attacks and vulnerabilities. Additionally, users should consider using third-party auditing services to review the code of smart contracts before executing them.

Finally, users should be prepared to take swift action in the event of a security breach or other issue with a smart contract. This may involve reporting the issue to the platform operator, seeking legal recourse, or taking other measures to protect their interests.

Overall, while smart contracts offer numerous benefits, they also pose potential risks that users should be aware of. By taking the necessary precautions and staying vigilant, users can help ensure the security and integrity of their smart contract-based transactions.

Chapter 6: When All Else Fails: Reporting Fraudulent Activity on the Blockchain

Part 1: Understanding the Importance of Reporting Fraudulent Activity

The blockchain technology has brought about a new era of trust and transparency in the digital world. However, despite its many benefits, it is not completely immune to fraudulent activity. From hacks and thefts to scams and Ponzi schemes, there are several ways in which malicious actors can exploit the system for their own gain.

The decentralized nature of the blockchain makes it difficult to regulate and monitor transactions. Unlike traditional financial institutions, there is no central authority that can oversee the network and protect users from fraudulent activity. This makes it crucial for users to take responsibility for their own security and report any suspicious activity they come across.

Reporting fraudulent activity not only helps protect individual users but also helps maintain the integrity of the blockchain network as a whole. By reporting such activity, users can prevent others from falling victim to similar scams and help law enforcement agencies track down and prosecute those responsible.

In this chapter, we will discuss the various types of fraudulent activity that can occur on the blockchain, the importance of reporting such activity, and the steps users can take to do so effectively. We will also explore the role of law enforcement agencies in investigating and prosecuting blockchain-related crimes.

Part 2: Identifying scams and fraudulent activity

As with any new technology, there are always those who seek to take advantage of its novelty and lack of regulation. The blockchain is no exception. Scammers are constantly devising new and creative ways to deceive unsuspecting victims into sending them money or sharing sensitive information.

In this section, we'll explore some of the most common scams and fraudulent activities on the blockchain and offer tips on how to identify and avoid them.

Phishing Scams

Phishing scams are one of the most common forms of online fraud, and the blockchain is no exception. In a typical phishing scam, a fraudster will send an email or message that appears to be from a legitimate source, such as a blockchain platform or a cryptocurrency exchange. The message will typically ask the recipient to click on a link or download an attachment, which will then install malware on their device or redirect them to a fake website where they will be prompted to enter sensitive information such as their private keys or login credentials.

To avoid falling victim to phishing scams, it's important to always double-check the sender's email address and the URL of any links or attachments before clicking on them. If the email or message seems suspicious, it's best to delete it immediately and not engage with the sender.

Ponzi Schemes

Ponzi schemes are a type of investment scam in which investors are promised high returns on their investment, but the returns are paid out using the capital of new investors rather than from actual profits. Eventually, the scheme collapses when there are no more new investors to pay out the returns, and the original investors lose their money.

On the blockchain, Ponzi schemes are often disguised as legitimate investment opportunities, such as initial coin offerings (ICOs) or high-yield investment programs (HYIPs). To avoid falling victim to a Ponzi scheme, it's important to thoroughly research any investment opportunities before investing. Look for reviews and feedback from other investors and be wary of any opportunity that promises unrealistic returns.

Fake Wallets and Exchanges

Fake wallets and exchanges are another common form of fraud on the blockchain. In a fake wallet scam, a fraudster will create a fake wallet app or website that appears to be legitimate but is actually designed to steal the user's private keys or other sensitive information. In a fake exchange scam, the fraudster will create a fake cryptocurrency exchange that appears to be legitimate but is actually designed to steal the user's cryptocurrency or other funds.

To avoid falling victim to fake wallet and exchange scams, it's important to only use reputable and well-established wallets and exchanges. Do your research and read reviews from other users before entrusting your funds to any platform.

Malware and Ransomware

Malware and ransomware are types of malicious software that are designed to infect a user's device and steal their sensitive information, or to encrypt their files and demand a ransom payment in exchange for the decryption key. On the blockchain, malware and ransomware can be used to steal a user's private keys or to encrypt their cryptocurrency wallets.

To avoid falling victim to malware and ransomware attacks, it's important to keep your device's software and antivirus programs up to date, and to avoid downloading or installing any suspicious software or files.

In conclusion, there are many different types of scams and fraudulent activities on the blockchain, and it's important to be aware of them in order to protect yourself and your funds. Always be cautious when sharing sensitive information or investing in any new opportunity and be sure to do your research before entrusting your funds to any platform or wallet.

Part 3: Reporting Fraudulent Activity to the Appropriate Authorities

Reporting Fraudulent Activity to the Appropriate Authorities

It can be a daunting task to report fraudulent activity on the blockchain. However, it's important to remember that there are steps you can take to ensure that the appropriate authorities are informed of any fraudulent activity that you come across. In this section, we will discuss the different ways you can report fraudulent activity and who to contact in such situations.

The first thing to do when you come across fraudulent activity on the blockchain is to document everything. This includes taking screenshots, saving any relevant links or messages, and writing down any important details such as transaction IDs, dates, and amounts. The more information you have, the easier it will be to provide evidence of the fraudulent activity.

Once you have documented everything, the next step is to contact the appropriate authorities. The authorities you should contact will depend on the type of fraudulent activity you have come across. For example, if you have come across an investment scam, you may need to contact the Securities and Exchange Commission (SEC) or the Financial Industry Regulatory Authority (FINRA). If you have come across a Ponzi scheme, you may need to contact the Federal Bureau of Investigation (FBI) or the Federal Trade Commission (FTC).

It's important to note that not all fraudulent activity on the blockchain will fall under the jurisdiction of these agencies. For example, if you have come across a scam involving a cryptocurrency wallet, you may need to contact the wallet provider or the cryptocurrency exchange involved.

When contacting the appropriate authorities, be sure to provide as much information as possible. This includes any documentation you have collected, as well as a detailed description of the fraudulent activity. The more information you can provide, the better the chances of the authorities being able to take action.

It's also important to be patient. Reporting fraudulent activity on the blockchain can take time, and the authorities may need to investigate the situation before taking any action. However, by reporting the activity, you are doing your part to help prevent others from falling victim to the same scam.

In addition to reporting fraudulent activity to the authorities, you can also report it to the blockchain community. Many blockchain communities have forums and chat rooms where users can discuss fraudulent activity and warn others about potential scams. By sharing your experience, you can help others avoid falling victim to the same scam.

Finally, it's important to stay vigilant when using blockchain-based platforms. While fraudulent activity can be reported and prevented, it's always better to be proactive and avoid falling victim to scams in the first place. This means staying informed about the latest scams and using caution when dealing with unfamiliar individuals or platforms.

In conclusion, reporting fraudulent activity on the blockchain is an important step in protecting yourself and others from scams and fraud. By documenting the activity, contacting the appropriate authorities, and sharing your experience with the community, you can help prevent others from falling victim to the same scam. Remember to stay vigilant and informed to avoid becoming a victim of fraudulent activity in the first place.

Part 4: The future of blockchain security: What's next?

As blockchain technology continues to evolve, so too does the field of blockchain security. While the industry has made significant strides in protecting users from fraud and theft, there is always room for improvement.

One area where we can expect to see continued progress is in the development of more sophisticated security measures. As blockchain-based applications become more complex and diverse, the need for more robust security protocols becomes increasingly important. This is particularly true when it comes to smart contracts, which are essentially self-executing programs that carry out specific tasks on the blockchain.

One potential solution that has been proposed is the use of "formal verification" techniques. These techniques involve mathematically proving the correctness of a smart contract before it is deployed on the blockchain. This would provide an extra layer of security, as any flaws or vulnerabilities in the contract's code would be identified and fixed before it could be exploited.

Another area of innovation that we can expect to see in the coming years is the development of decentralized identity solutions. These solutions would allow users to maintain control over their own identity data, rather than relying on centralized authorities such as governments or social media platforms. By using the blockchain to create a decentralized identity network, users would be able to more securely and easily manage their personal information and reduce the risk of identity theft or fraud.

One potential drawback of these new security measures, however, is that they may make the blockchain less accessible to everyday users. As security becomes more sophisticated and complex, it may become increasingly difficult for non-experts to use and understand blockchain-based applications. To address this, the industry will need to find ways to balance security with ease of use and accessibility.

In addition to technological innovations, there are also likely to be new regulatory and legal frameworks developed to address blockchain security issues. As the technology continues to gain mainstream adoption, governments and regulatory bodies around the world are taking a closer look at how they can ensure that blockchain-based applications are safe and secure for users.

Finally, we can expect to see continued collaboration and cooperation within the blockchain industry to address security challenges. As the saying goes, "a rising tide lifts all boats." By working together to develop and implement new security measures, blockchain developers, businesses, and users can all benefit from a more secure and trustworthy ecosystem.

In conclusion, while the blockchain has certainly brought with it new security challenges and risks, it has also sparked a wave of innovation and development in the field of blockchain security. As we move forward, we can expect to see continued progress in this area, driven by technological advancements, regulatory frameworks, and collaboration within the industry. With a combination of innovative solutions and common-sense best practices, we can continue to enjoy the benefits of the blockchain while minimizing the risks.

Appendix: Blockchain Jargon Buster

A playful guide to decoding the most common blockchain terms and jargon.

Are you feeling lost in a sea of blockchain buzzwords and technical terms? Fear not, dear reader! This appendix is here to provide you with a playful guide to decoding some of the most common blockchain terms and jargon.

Blockchain: A decentralized, digital ledger that records transactions across a network of computers. Each block on the chain contains a cryptographic hash of the previous block, creating an unbreakable chain of information.

Cryptocurrency: A digital or virtual currency that uses cryptography for security. Bitcoin, Ethereum, and Litecoin are some of the most well-known cryptocurrencies.

Mining: The process by which new blocks are added to the blockchain. Miners use powerful computers to solve complex mathematical equations and are rewarded with new cryptocurrency for their efforts.

Wallet: A digital wallet is a software program that stores public and private keys and interacts with various blockchain networks to enable users to send, receive, and manage their digital assets.

Private Key: A secret code that allows users to access their cryptocurrency wallet and make transactions on the blockchain.

Public Key: A public code that is used to receive cryptocurrency transactions. It can be shared with others without compromising security.

Smart Contract: A self-executing contract with the terms of the agreement between buyer and seller being directly written into lines of code. Smart contracts are used to automate the execution of transactions on the blockchain.

ICO: Initial Coin Offering. A fundraising method in which new cryptocurrency projects sell their tokens in exchange for established cryptocurrencies like Bitcoin or Ethereum.

Hash: A unique digital fingerprint that is created through complex mathematical algorithms and is used to verify the authenticity and integrity of data on the blockchain.

Consensus: The agreement between all the nodes on the blockchain network on the validity of a transaction or block. Consensus is essential to maintain the security and integrity of the blockchain.

Fork: A split in the blockchain caused by differences in opinion among the network's users or developers. Forks can result in the creation of a new blockchain with different rules and features.

Gas: A unit used to measure the amount of computational power required to execute a smart contract on the blockchain. Users must pay gas fees in order to use the network.

Node: A computer or device that participates in the blockchain network by storing, validating, and broadcasting transactions and blocks.

Private Blockchain: A blockchain that is operated by a single entity, such as a company or organization, and is not open to public participation.

Public Blockchain: A blockchain that is open to anyone to participate and access, such as the Bitcoin or Ethereum networks.

Consensus Algorithm - The mechanism by which a blockchain network validates transactions and achieves agreement on the state of the ledger. Examples include Proof of Work, Proof of Stake, and Delegated Proof of Stake.

Gas - A unit of measurement used to determine the cost of executing a transaction on the Ethereum network. The more complex the transaction, the more gas it requires and the higher the fee.

Fork - A split in the blockchain caused by a disagreement among participants in the network. There are two types of forks: soft forks, which are backwards compatible with previous versions of the blockchain, and hard forks, which require all participants to upgrade to the new version.

Node - A computer that is connected to a blockchain network and helps validate transactions by maintaining a copy of the ledger.

Smart Contract - A self-executing contract that automatically enforces the terms of an agreement when certain conditions are met. Smart contracts are programmed in code and run on the blockchain, making them transparent, immutable, and tamper-proof.

Wallet - A software program that stores public and private keys and allows users to send and receive cryptocurrencies. Wallets can be hot (connected to the internet) or cold (offline) and come in various forms, including desktop, mobile, and hardware.

Token - A unit of value that is issued and managed on a blockchain network. Tokens can represent anything of value, including currency, assets, or utility.

Mining - The process of adding new blocks to the blockchain by solving complex mathematical problems. Miners are rewarded with new cryptocurrency for their efforts.

ICO - An initial coin offering, a fundraising mechanism used by blockchain startups to raise capital in exchange for newly issued tokens.

Private Key - A secret code that is used to access a user's cryptocurrency holdings. It is essential to keep private keys safe and secure, as they grant full access to the associated funds.

Don't miss out!

Visit the website below and you can sign up to receive emails whenever Michael Ferguson publishes a new book. There's no charge and no obligation.

https://books2read.com/r/B-A-CKNW-QFHHC

Connecting independent readers to independent writers.

Did you love *Blockchain Gold Rush: Surviving The Wild Wild West of Decentralization*? Then you should read *Prompt Engineering ; The Future Of Language Generation*[1] by Michael Ferguson!

"AI Prompt Engineering: The Future of Language Generation" is a book that covers the cutting-edge field of AI-powered language generation, from the basics of AI prompt engineering to advanced techniques and best practices for building intelligent chatbots and other conversational systems. Written with the help of experts in the field, the book covers fundamental concepts and technologies such as NLP and ML, techniques and tools used in AI-powered language generation systems, practical examples, case studies, ethical and social implications and future possibilities of the field. It's a must-read for anyone interested in the development and application of AI-powered

1. https://books2read.com/u/b6VKB6

2. https://books2read.com/u/b6VKB6

language generation technology, whether developers, researchers or anyone with a passion for technology.

www.ingramcontent.com/pod-product-compliance
Lightning Source LLC
Chambersburg PA
CBHW052100150726

48002CB00002B/962